LifeCap

# The True Story of the Jersey Boys

*The Story Behind Frankie Valli and the Four Seasons*

By Jennifer Warner

BookCaps™ Study Guides

www.bookcaps.com

# Table of Contents

# About LifeCaps

LifeCaps is an imprint of BookCaps™ Study Guides. With each book, a lesser known or sometimes forgotten life is recapped. We publish a wide array of topics (from baseball and music to literature and philosophy), so check our growing catalogue regularly (www.bookcaps.com) to see our newest books.

## Disclosure

*While the contents of this biography have been researched, this book is not endorsed or affiliated in anyway with  Frankie Valli or The Four Seasons.*

# Chapter 1: Introduction

Frank Sinatra dazzled a lot of people with his crooning, but for Frankie Valli, Sinatra was not just a great voice.

Valli was only seven years old when his mother took him to a Sinatra concert at the Paramount Theater in New York City. What struck the young boy was not just the beauty of Sinatra's voice, but the way he understood and got to the heart of the lyrics. The bright lights, the roar of the crowd all had a hypnotic and unforgettable effect on the young Valli. The stage, he reminisces, seemed like it was a hundred feet above his head.

Sinatra had an aura and right then, at seven years of age, Valli wanted to become a professional singer.

That concert may have been the first building block in what became Frankie Valli's long, sensational career. But Sinatra was not the only jazz legend that Valli learned from. Growing up in Newark, New Jersey, Valli was surrounded by jazz.

In the 1920s, Newark was alive with entertainment. Sixty-three live theaters and a thriving music scene rooted in pubs and nightclubs made the city buzz. By the 1940s, when Valli was a young man, the city had lost a lot of its luster. Bad urban planning precipitated the flight of more affluent residents while their places were taken by struggling immigrants. Valli was born into one such family.

But the city was still rich in music. People would gather spontaneously in the streets and harmonize under the street lights or under bridges. Groups of friends would burst into song in pool halls. Valli would play hooky from school to hear concerts in downtown Newark.

Valli would lower the volume of his radio to a light whisper so that he could continue listening to music all through the night and well into the early morning, often drifting between waking and sleeping. He stayed up to listen to Symphony Sid, in particular, because that radio celebrity's show went from midnight to six AM.

It was an ideal atmosphere for a self-taught musician such as Valli would become.

Growing up in this musical bubble, Valli wanted to participate from an early age. He bought songbooks that had the lyrics of songs he heard on the radio. Using the songbooks, he would sing along to the recorded greats, often imitating their styles and discovering that he could do a broad range of different things with his voice.

Looking back, Valli notes that this was better training than going to a singing coach because the students of any particular coach all sound the same. That's how they've been coached to sound.

"But by doing impressions, you can broaden that scope," Valli told a National Public Radio interviewer much, much later. "There will be more possibilities when you're singing."

Valli says he was a "jazz freak" who listened avidly to vocal groups like the Four Freshmen, the Hi-Los, and the Modernaires. On any day that Newark did not provide the musical stimulation Valli craved, New York City was only five miles away. New York's legendary Birdland Club featured a neon sign saying "Birdland, Jazz Corner of the World. There, celebrities rubbed shoulders with the most famous singers of the time. Some of the greatest jazz albums were recorded there, live.

Valli could not have asked for a better incubator in which to become a music legend in his own right. He spent whole days in Birdland. He swooned to the vocal talents of Yma Sumac, a singer from Peru with a five-octave range. He soaked up the music of Dinah Washington, Nat King Cole, Count Basie, and Stan Kenton.

It was during this formative time in Valli's life that he also heard "Little" Jimmy Scott, a jazz singer with an abnormally high contralto caused by Kallmann's Syndrome. Kallmann's stunted Scott's growth so that his voice never matured. His choirboy-like sound is more than likely one of the influences on the falsetto that helped make Valli famous.

When he wasn't at Birdland, Valli often haunted a pool hall in Belleville, but not so much to play pool. Instead, he found someone with a guitar and jammed. During this time, Valli met Nick Massi. Massi encouraged Valli to develop his talent as a musician and the two eventually became bandmates in the Four Seasons.

Jazz was Valli's first musical love and he has been known to say that he never intended to become a rock and roll star. But rock and roll was the pathway to commercial success in the 1960s when Valli came into his own as a musician, and he rolled with it.

Valli is the son of Anthony Castelluccio, a barber who later became a display designer for Lionel model trains and Mary Rinaldi who was, for the most part, a full-time mother though she worked for a while in the beer making industry. He was the youngest of three sons. The name his parents gave him was Fran20cesco Stephen Castelluccio, a handle even his earliest agents could not wrap a career around, so they renamed him. Valli tried out several monikers on the way to settling down with one. First, he shortened his name to Valley, after his mentor Jean Valley. Later, he put some of the Italian immigrant back into it with "Valli."

Depending on who you ask, Valli was born in 1934 or 1937. On his rise to stardom, he may have shaved three official years off his age in order to increase his appeal to the young audiences he intended to reach. There is an ongoing uncertainty about his exact age.

He grew up in Newark's first ward. His family lived for years off Garside Avenue in an unheated apartment with no hot water. They kept warm in winter with a wood stove and many blankets.

When he was six, the Castelluccio family moved to the Stephen Crane Village which, despite its poetic name, was actually a housing development subsidized by the state. Valli attended Abington Avenue School and later Central High.

By 1950, when Valli was sixteen (or thirteen), Newark had already lost its foothold as an important and thriving hub of manufacturing and transportation. Valli's prospects in his poor Newark neighborhood looked grim. His father informed him that there would be no college experience waiting for him after high school. Many of Valli's friends got absorbed into local organized crime, some of them achieving leadership positions in the mafia. By his own testimony, Valli knew people who ended up dead in the trunks of cars, the victims of mob violence. The only path to honest work seemed to be low-wage jobs in manufacturing or retail.

And that was certainly the path his father encouraged. Mr. Castelluccio did not at first believe that Valli could make a living as a musician. He urged young Frankie to get a real job and settle down.

Valli admits to getting himself into trouble as a young man in Newark. His community and the young people growing up in it were beset with a sense of futility, a lack of confidence that they could escape what was a crime culture. Valli says his community was "nowhere near middle class." Most of his friends never got an education past high school. Many, like Valli himself, dropped out.

He was arrested once for breaking and entering. He got in fights. But his life of aimless trouble making came to an abrupt end when he came home one night, bruised and battered from a conflict with the police. His father, who rarely let slip an emotion, cried when he saw how hurt Valli was.

"When I saw him cry, that was the end of my getting in trouble," Valli said.

Valli's rough childhood and early manhood haunted him as a musician because he was afraid that if his fan base learned of his less than pristine background, he would fail.

"The one thing that I was afraid of more than anything was that the public might find out we were not clean-cut kids who went to church every Sunday," Valli said in an interview decades later. "Some of the guys in the group had prison records. So we just prayed and hoped that nobody would ever find out."

In a world where the mafia had a very real, not fictitious presence, Valli, like Sinatra, walked a fine line between accepting friendship and protection and becoming part of the mob. It was a line he managed never to cross, even though he admits to a close friendship with famed mobster Angelo "Gyp" DeCarlo. Valli says DeCarlo was like a second father when Valli was a young man coming up in Newark.

Valli started singing at a young age and became known around his neighborhood for having an "angel voice." He got his first big break when a country singer, "Texas" Jean Valley, heard him sing "White Christmas" in a school play.

Today, little is known about Jean Valley, known in her day for a unique rendition of "World's

About To Lose (Its Biggest Fool)," except that she took the very young Valli under her wing, passed him off as her little brother, and helped him launch his music career. In honor of her, Valli later took her last name as his stage name.

Valli dropped out of high school over the objections of his father. He briefly took up his father's trade, barbering, in order to support himself. But he left the scissors and comb to take his chances as a musician. Music offered what seemed the only chance for a bigger life for someone from a rough Newark neighborhood.

Tommy DeVito and Nick Massi, who would later become the Four Lovers and then the Four Seasons along with Valli, lived in Newark, and Valli knew them when he was growing up because they, too, managed to get into scrapes with the law. One thing they agreed on was that they wanted to make it in music, not the mob.

In those days, television was gaining ground as everyman's entertainment, but it offered nothing for night owls. After 11:00 PM, the set went to white noise, and people who wanted to socialize and stay up late went to bars, many of which featured very rudimentary music scenes.

Valli's earliest paid gig was in one such establishment, the Club Rendezvous, a no-frills bar where the owner had decided to offer live music. The set up could not have been less luxurious. There was no stage, few tables and chairs. The band played behind the bar for a standing audience. The band performed four or five sets a night for the sum of five to eight dollars. A better gig was one that paid room and board at Jazz City on the Jersey shore, but it was summer work only.

In 1951, Valli joined a band called the Variety Trio which was organized around the talents of Tommy DeVito. Valli became a member after one night when Tommy DeVito, who headed the Variety Trio, invited Valli on stage to perform with them. Valli sang "I Can't Give You Anything But Love." On that night, a lasting partnership would be formed. Valli and DeVito stuck together through their years to come in the Variatones, the Four Lovers, and the Four Seasons.

By Valli's own account, the Variety Trio made little money and it broke up after approximately a year, but Valli continued to play with DeVito and together they formed a new band, the Variatones with Hank Majewski, Frank Cattone and Billy Thompson.

In 1953, at only nineteen years of age, Valli signed a contract with Corona, a subsidiary of Mercury Records which released his first single, a rendition of "My Mother's Eyes" by Georgie Jessel. A year later, he recorded "Forgive and Forget" with the same company. Neither song propelled Valli into stardom.

Frankie Valli did not become the band's front man until quite a bit later when the hit "Sherry" pushed him to the front. Tommy DeVito dominated the Variety Trio, grabbing the lion's share of the group's slim income until the other group members mutinied and demanded a more equal share of earnings.

Bootstrapping a musical career on the Jersey shore meant taking a job where you could find it and playing long hours for little money. It also meant frequent trips to the Brill Building in Manhattan, the virtual center of the music writing and publishing business where Valli and his fellow musicians would venture to make demos of their sound.

The Brill Building was already the established hotbed of popular music before World War II. By the time Valli's star was rising, it was the go-to place to meet music producers, get recorded, and take your chances with fame. Eleven stories tall, the Brill housed rehearsal rooms and cubby holes for writers. As a struggling unknown, Valli pounded its halls, hearing music that overflowed from every room. Frankie Valli and the Four Seasons would eventually be headquartered in the Brill Building.

Prior to the runaway success of the Four Seasons, however, the Variatones floundered, members came and went and the band tried out a series of different names including The Romans, The Topics, and The Village Voices. In a 21st century interview, Valli said there were other names, but they were inappropriate for radio.

# Chapter 2: The Four Lovers

Midway between starving in a garret and cresting on superstardom, the Variatones morphed into the Four Lovers. Rechristened, the group's fortunes started to rise, but slowly. They started recording on the RCA label. Their first record "You're the Apple of My Eye," made it to number 62 on the Billboard Hot 100. This hit got them a spot on the coveted Ed Sullivan show in 1956. Dressed in matching black suits, string ties, and shoes polished into virtual mirrors, the Four Lovers delivered a pitch-perfect performance of their hit without missing a note or a dance step.

Despite their flawless performance on Ed Sullivan, for a few more years, it looked like the Four Lovers would be a one-hit wonder. RCA dropped the Four Lovers when they did not produce another hit. Epic signed them, but also dropped them for the same reason.

By 1957, they had recorded six other songs, tunes that evaporated into the air waves, getting little if any radio play or attention.

The Four Lovers got a break when two talents were added to their plate: Producer Bob Crewe, known for an unerring ear for music and Bob Gaudio. Gaudio was a multi-talented musician proficient at the keyboard, guitar, and vocals as well as writing new music. Gaudio brought a harmonic element to the band that it had been sorely missing, and the group's sound crystallized with his talent and Crewe's direction.

By some accounts Gaudio and Valli were introduced by Joe Pesci who would himself become famous as an actor and Academy Award Oscar winner for his role in *Good Fellas*.

Gaudio and Valli formed a nearly instantaneous mutual admiration society. Gaudio had first heard Valli sing at the Silhouette Club. Valli sang "Moody's Mood for Love," a song usually performed as a duet by a man and a woman. Valli, using his falsetto, performed both parts, putting a handkerchief on his head when he segued into the female role. Gaudio was astounded by Valli's range.

For his part, Valli admired Gaudio's writing. "I was quite sure that he was the guy that I should hook up with," Valli said. "He thought a lot the way I did; he was a doer, not just a talker." Valli's friendship with Gaudio became a collaboration that benefitted them both for decades to come. They remain friends and business partners for over fifty years.

Bob Crewe signed the Four Lovers for three years and paid them $15 per recorded demo. Their contracts allowed the band members freedom to work on solo projects as they felt led. As the Four Lovers, the band could get session work to supplement their income from singing lounges and clubs. They frequently played back to other bands that Crewe was promoting.

Nevertheless, Valli reports that, even at this point in his career, he was not a full-time musician. He had a day job working maintenance for the City of Newark.

The success of the Four Lovers was uneven under Crewe's direction, but the band did acquire an in-house composer and arranger, freeing them from having to solicit new songs from other musicians. However, the added infrastructure did not guarantee their success. The death knell for the Lovers came when they auditioned at a bowling alley cocktail lounge in

Union, New Jersey and did not get the gig. Because that dismal failure came at the end of their contract, the group disbanded and Bob Gaudio and Frankie Valli formed a new band which would commemorate their defeat in the bowling alley. The name of that bowling alley cocktail lounge was "The Four Seasons."

Valli and Gaudio made a handshake deal to share each other's fortunes until death did them part, and few marriages have been as successful in fulfilling their participants' commitment. Gaudio agreed that he would split every penny he made on his writing and performances, and Valli agreed to split all his earnings, both from work he did with Gaudio and solo work. The musicians have stuck to that agreement to this day without a contract.

The Four Lovers were dead. Long live the Four Seasons.

# Chapter 3: The Four Seasons

In 1960, Gaudio and Valli shook hands to seal their agreement on a new band, the Four Seasons. By 1961, they had recorded "Bermuda/Spanish Lace" for Gone Records. The song did not make it to the charts.

The Four Seasons initially found that they did not get far without Bob Crewe. So they started working for him again, doing session and back-up work.

Valli's life at this point was a broad circuit of lounges and tours. Unlike many big stars, he never despised these small gigs, and never thought of himself contemptuously as a lounge lizard. Looking back on his career many years later, he claimed that he would have been happy and contented in life just being a successful lounge performer.

"I enjoyed a lot of what I did in those days," he told the *Washington Post*. "I think back sometimes how nice it would be to work in a lounge where you didn't have to do a set show and you did what you felt like doing."

Touring in the early 1960s was very different from what it is today. For one thing, Valli notes, he did not make the kind of money on tour that musical celebrities today make.

Valli praises the warmth and camaraderie that he found when he was on tour. He found it easy to make close friends with the other musicians on the rhythm and blues circuit. They looked out for each other. If one of the acts fell under the weather, another performer would cover for him.

They ate and slept and socialized on the bus, going from town to town. And when they pulled into a new destination, the band would visit all the radio stations in that town to give interviews and talk to the disc jockeys about their music.

"Today, performers make 50 times the kind of money we made in those days and they won't go to a radio station, they take on an attitude that I can't quite understand," Valli says.

Even as big stars, Valli and his colleagues were generously interactive with their audiences. A 1968 advertisement for a Four Seasons concert, which ran in the *New York Times,* notes that the musicians will be available to sign albums, all of which are available for the affordable price of $2.69. Their 45 hit of that moment was only fifty-nine cents. They were signing those, too.

The tide turned one night when the Four Seasons played at a nightclub in Point Pleasant. Bob Crewe was present, and the band gave a thirty-minute performance which was followed by a small impromptu jam session. For no apparent reason, Valli started singing the jazz standard "I can't give you anything but love, baby" in the voice of Rose Murphy, sometimes known as the "chee chee girl."

Valli's spoof on the song involved folding a napkin into a hat which he put on his head, holding maracas in front of his chest to signify breasts, and singing "I can't give you anything but love, chee chee" in a false soprano.

Crewe was anything but annoyed. He was intrigued. He turned to Bob Gaudio and said that he should write something for that voice. "I don't care what it's about; just incorporate an octave jump from the high falsetto to the low baritone and back, low to high," said Crew. "It will be phenomenal."

That, according to legend, is how the song "Sherry" was born.

Gaudio claims he popped out the tune at his piano in fifteen minutes of down time between recording sessions. He describes the lyrics as silly, but they depict "everyone that I knew, any girl I had dated."

Crewe says the song was a turning point in his career, too. Recording "Sherry" was a gamble for him because he had to set aside the work that paid his bills to record this new song by a still fledgling band. "I took a chance that my mother and father would pay my rent that month," he says. He sensed right away that the song was a potentially huge hit, the kind of song that will rocket to the top of the charts. He felt like the demo was burning a hole in his pocket as he transported it to Miami to pitch it to some music producers there.

In an interview with the *Washington Post*, Valli said that "Sherry" was all about establishing an attention-grabbing style. He knew that the song would strike gold or strike out. It was such a new sound, there was really no in between.

On September 15, 1962, Crewe's hunch about "Sherry" was vindicated. It did go to number one on the Billboard Hot 100 list and it stayed there for five weeks.

Writing the tune and lyrics took only minutes, but the song underwent a great deal of 1960s mixing before it became the huge hit that everyone was humming in the shower. Charlie Callelo, the Four Seasons' arranger computed an almost mathematical formula for what makes a song a hit. The successful brew, he concluded, is a song that incorporates a girl's name in the title, big production values, and some boy-on-girl romantic begging. "Sherry" was adjusted to accommodate all these market features. The twist was the dance craze of the moment, so in "Sherry," Valli's flexible voice implores Sherry to come to a twist party.

"Sherry" was the single most important turning point in Frankie Valli's career, because it pushed him to the front of the stage. His name featured prominently in the buzz surrounding the hit song. In promoting "Sherry," producers referred to the band as the "Four Seasons featuring The Sound Of Frankie Valli."

Using "Sherry" as leverage, the Four Seasons finally got a record label with Vee Jay Records, a Black-owned record label that had only one prior hit. The Four Seasons had, until that moment, been considered a sort of anomalous rhythm and blues band featuring white boys. Their sound was also classed as "doo-wop" at the point in history when doo-wop was going the way of the dodo. When it got any radio play at all, the Four Seasons were heard on Black-owned radio stations with mostly Black listeners.

So when it came to getting "Sherry" out to the public ear, Valli approached Randy Wood who worked for Vee Jay Records on the west coast. Wood listened to the song and gave a copy to a local radio disc jockey named Dick "Huggy Boy" Hugg. When Hugg's listeners heard "Sherry," they started jamming the phone lines with requests to hear it again, and Vee Jay promptly cut a record.

From there, "Sherry" crossed over into the world of music lovers who were dancing to the Beatles and Elvis Presley. By the time "Sherry" was played on television, the Four Seasons had made the transition to the pop/rock category.

On December 9th, 1962, the band returned to the Ed Sullivan show to perform "Sherry" and this time, they won the hearts of America's music lovers. A full album followed, titled "Sherry and 11 Others" (meaning eleven other songs). The album went to number 6 on Billboard Music Week's Top LP's.

Through the next decades, there would be diverse opinions about Valli's falsetto. Teenage girls often swooned and radio listeners demanded more of that sound. Die-hard fans sang along, sometimes filling whole auditoriums with the sound of a thousand falsettos. Others remained unconvinced of the artistry, at times accusing Valli of singing through his nose or sounding like a "freak" or "Mickey Mouse on helium." Valli himself joked that he sounded like Betty Boop.

The Billboard Hot 100 list was, in 1962, a relatively new but popular instrument for measuring the success of popular songs. *Billboard Magazine* had started publishing the Hot 100 in August of 1958, only four years previous to the release of "Sherry." The magazine used the objective measurements of radio play time and sales to pinpoint which songs were the most popular on any given week. Despite its newness, audiences quickly came to trust the Hot 100, and it contributed to the snowballing fame that the Four Seasons acquired in the next three years.

Valli was not one of those celebrities who make a fortune and quickly blow it on cars and women. Instead, he was cautious of his success. He didn't quit his day job, but instead renewed his contract to do maintenance work for another six months after "Sherry" took off. After all, he had a family to think of. When "Sherry" became a hit, Valli was already married to Mary Mandel who had a daughter, Celia, from a prior relationship. Valli and Mandel would be united for thirteen years. He raised Celia as his own and they had two more daughters, Toni and Francine.

"I was afraid that, if this all went away, how would I be able to pay for anything?" he says.

After the runaway success of "Sherry," he waited a full two years before buying a car. He waited another year after that before buying a house.

His career had, after all, been a rapid succession of highs and lows, never the kind of support beam on which to rest the future.

But this time, Valli's success did not fade away as quickly as it arrived. "Sherry" was not a one-off hit. The Four Seasons followed up on it with many other hit songs. The next one was "Big Girls Don't Cry," which they released just as "Sherry" was losing its first-place foothold on the Hot 100 list.

There are two different stories about how "Big Girls Don't Cry" was born. Both Gaudio and Crewe have, at different points, claimed credit for the original idea, though they agree that the song was actually written by Gaudio.

Both claim to have been inspired by a John Payne and Rhonda Fleming movie.

Gaudio claims to have been drifting in and out of sleep while watching *Tennessee's Partner*. He woke up at the point in the movie where Payne slaps Fleming and wrote down the words "Big girls don't cry." The liner notes to *Frankie Valli & the Four Seasons'* "The Rock 'N' Roll Era" published by Time-Life Records in 1987 tell that story, but the story falls apart because no scene in Tennessee's Partner actually includes that line.

Crewe's story is more likely. He admits to doing quite a bit of drinking at that time. He had poured himself a drink and retired to his upstairs library to pass out. He awoke when there was a ruckus on the television set and Payne was, once again, manhandling Fleming. The movie was *Slightly Scarlet*. In *Slightly Scarlet*, however, Payne actually says "Big girls don't cry."

Crewe says he was so excited about this seed for a new song that he could hardly wait for the sun to come up. He pitched the song title to Gaudio and he wrote it the next day.

"Big Girls Don't Cry," like "Sherry," leveraged Valli's now-famous falsetto, and the Four Seasons had a second hit. "Big Girls Don't Cry" spent another five weeks at the top of the Billboard Hot 100 list. An album titled "Big Girls Don't Cry and 12 Others" followed on the heels of this second hit. As the album title suggests, the hit song was the heart of the album along with twelve other songs that were of interest to fans, but not on a loop at most radio stations. In the same year, the Four Seasons even found time to pump out a Christmas album which featured a new interpretation of "Santa Claus Is Coming to Town."

The next hit that the Four Seasons produced was "Walk Like a Man" in 1963. Marshall Brickman, the famous screenwriter and Woody Allen collaborator, once said that the Four Seasons' songbook isn't really so much about boys singing to girls. It's more about boys complaining about girls to other boys. In no song is this more obvious than "Walk Like a Man," in which a father tells his son to get over being dumped. "Walk Like a Man" pitted Valli's falsetto against Nick Massi's deep bass vocals.

Valli and Gaudio continued to nurture each other's talents, and their bond grew stronger. Valli says, "Our friendship became tighter and the things that we wanted were incredibly similar .... You nourish each other with creative thoughts that evolve into bigger things."

Gaudio, unlike Valli, was less cautious about taking the startling success of the Four Seasons to the bank. He bought a house in Montclair that he describes as "ridiculously big" with twenty-eight bedrooms and designed by one of the geniuses behind the Empire State Building. Though Valli did immediately immerse himself in similar luxury, he often relaxed by the pool at Gaudio's mansion where a party was often in session.

Valli's fame also attracted the welcome companionship of other music legends of the time. He admired and wanted to meet the Beatles, but found that they were surrounded by an impenetrable wall of managers and agents. On a whim, he called them up when they were in Italy and ended up hanging out with them in a hotel room. He also became friends with his childhood idol, Frank Sinatra.

Valli had been working with Sinatra's mother on a concert that raised money for blind children, and he first met Sinatra at Jilly's, a New York nightclub owned by Jilly Rizzo. Many people believe Rizzo was Sinatra's closest friend. Valli and Sinatra had drinks and dinner together and became friends for ten years. They talked on the phone; they worked together in Las Vegas.

Asked if he gleaned any tips from Sinatra, Valli says that he let the legend know up front that he wanted their friendship to be just that--a friendship, not a mentorship. According to legend, Sinatra sent his private Lear jet to fetch the Four Seasons when he was feeling lonely. On other occasions, it would just be Valli, Sinatra, and Rizzo hanging out in Sinatra's Palm Springs house.

Writing songs may have come easily to Bob Gaudio and Bob Crewe, but "Walk Like a Man" was recorded under duress. The Seasons were recording the song in the Abbey Victoria Hotel where Stea-Phillips Recording Studios was headquartered. A fire broke out on the floor immediately above where the group was recording. When smoke and fire started seeping into their studio, they knew something was happening, but they didn't stop recording. Crew kept pushing for the perfect sound as they did take after take of the song. Fire fighters demanded that they vacate the hotel, at which point Crewe barricaded the door and kept recording. Finally, firemen broke into the room with axes and forcibly extracted the band. "Walk Like a Man" hit the top of Hot 100 on March 2, 1963 and stayed there for three weeks.

The Four Seasons had hit their peak at this point. They were holding their own against the Beatles, Nat King Cole, Tony Bennett, and Peter, Paul and Mary, all huge names that would go down in music history. By combining Valli's amazing voice with the talents of Bob Gaudio, Nick Massi, and Tom DeVito, they had created the magic formula.

Even though their sound was very different, the Four Seasons were such successful rivals with the Beatles that Vee Jay Records, the company that cut both groups' records in the early 1960s, published an album titled "The Four Seasons versus the Beatles--International Battle of the Century." Valli noted in an interview many years later that there was a chart on the back of the album that invited listeners to score the bands.

Larry Santos wrote "Candy Girl" which became the Four Seasons' next big hit. In "Candy Girl," Valli applied his falsetto to a song which is basically a tribute to a sweet girlfriend. The song brings the Four Seasons' trademark doo-wop sound and rhythm to what is essentially a ballad. "Candy Girl" made it to third place on the Billboard Hot 100. And it was still 1963, arguably the Four Seasons' most golden year.

The lyrics to these early Four Seasons smash hits get different reactions from different listeners. There is no question that audiences of the time resonated with both harmonies and snappy beat, but the lyrics were uncomplicated to the point of inviting later criticism, even from Valli himself who told a London Daily Mail reporter that the lyrics were far from intellectual.

That may have been the point, though. Valli and his band of redeemed roughnecks from New Jersey had that ineffable boy-next-door quality. Their music sounded like the way people talk on street corners, set to a beat and beautiful harmonics. As boys who had escaped the worst destinies available to poor lads from Newark, they represented the hopes and dreams of many working class teenagers. To the girls in that audience, they sounded like the cool boys at school. Only those school boys were annoying and aloof, where the Four Seasons were so emotionally available, singing the girls to sleep on the radio right next to their heads.

Some people think that the music of the Four Seasons is an everyman kind of sound and thought. Others call it naive, sweet, nostalgic. It is true that the Seasons never incorporated some of the coarser sexual allusions that one hears, for instance, in the Rolling Stones. They were rarely casual or direct about sex in their music. Their hits reflect the polite courtship rituals of the

1950s rather than the free love ethics that were emerging in the 1960s.

Despite that, some critics have called the Seasons' lyrics "sexist," even "misogynistic." By the exacting standards of the twenty-first century, perhaps some of them are.

"We were a ghetto group who posed no threat because a guy could come and see us with his best girl and say: 'I'm just like him.'"

For their next project, the Four Seasons departed from their usual formula of writing their own music and producing it under the meticulous eye of Bob Crewe. Their next hit was a cover of "Ain't That a Shame" which had been recorded by  Fats Domino and Dave Bartholomew in 1955. The Fats Domino interpretation of the song topped the Black Singles chart, then was immediately covered by Pat Boone who was almost successful in getting his producers to correct the song's grammar.

With "Ain't That a Shame," the Four Seasons' solid run of hits momentarily flickered. The song was successful, but not as wildly popular as their last four songs had been. It ascended to a respectable, but not dazzling 22nd place on the Hot 100 list.

The band did anything but rest on their laurels. The mid-1960s was a flurry of song writing, recording, and performing for the Four Seasons. 1964 found them busy producing and recording another hit, "Rag Doll." The song tells the story of a pretty, fragile young woman from a poor family. The narrator of the song is a boy who would like to reach out to her, but his family forbids it, telling him in effect that she is not good enough for him.

It could be argued that, in creating "Rag Doll," Massi, DeVito, and Valli who grew up around the same time on rough Newark streets invented a female version of themselves: social outcasts with poor financial prospects and few hopes of overcoming class barriers.

"Rag Doll" was another successful product of the Crewe/Gaudio collaboration. Gaudio says the idea for the song came to him when an unkempt girl with dirt on her face washed his car window for change. Routing around in his pockets, all he could find was a twenty-dollar bill, so he gave her that. Her surprise haunted him and compelled him to write the song.

At that point in time, popular music was most often purchased on 45s, small records that could fit only one song on each side. Typically, the flip side of a hit song featured another song by the same artist, but one his producers believed was less commercially viable. It was rare for two hits to be published on the same 45, because record producers made their money from hits. It made good business sense to make people buy two records if they wanted two hits.

The "Rag Doll" 45 was accidentally an exception. It featured the single "Silence Is Golden," also written by Crewe and Gaudio and showcasing Valli's falsetto in the refrain. Though "Silence Is Golden" was not one of the Four Seasons' greatest hits, it went on to be covered by an English band, The Tremeloes, for whom it became a top hit in the United Kingdom in 1967.

In the same year, the Four Seasons wrote and recorded "Born to Wander," and the next year they cut another album titled "The 4 Seasons Entertain You.

But there were some rumblings in the foundation that the Four Seasons ignored until it was no longer possible. Vee Jay Records was struggling financially as a result of losing a Trans-Global contract. Musicians signed to Vee Jay, including the Beatles and other high profile musicians felt that Vee Jay Records was not paying them the agreed-upon royalties. Vee Jay had just settled a lawsuit with the Beatles when the Four Seasons followed suit in court. They, too, believed they had not been paid in accordance with the terms of their contract. The Four Seasons left Vee Jay and took their business to Phillips Records, a subsidiary of Mercury Records.

The single "Dawn" ("Go Away") was a hostage in these negotiations. Another Gaudio/Crewe collaboration, "Dawn" was performed and recorded by the Four Seasons in 1963. But, when Vee Jay withheld royalties from the Four Seasons, they retaliated by withholding "Dawn" and some other master tapes which escalated the conflict.

In 1965, "Dawn" was released under the Phillips Records label and it went to number 3 on the Hot 100 list, but it failed to topple two other rock legends that were released the same year: the Beatles' "I Want to Hold Your Hand" and "She Loves You."

In "Dawn," the Four Seasons continued to develop the motif of frustrated romance that you hear in their other songs. Unlike the heroine of "Rag Doll," Dawn is a girl who could do better than the boy who is singing to her and telling her to go away because he is too poor. This time, Valli's falsetto communicates desperation and pleading.

In the same year, the group also released "Bye, Bye, Baby" ("Baby Goodbye") in which the singers' yearning for a woman is frustrated by his prior commitment to another woman.

Meanwhile, Nick Massi was not happy, and he left the band in 1965 with no real warning or explanation. The band was in the middle of a tour when this happened. Valli and his colleagues had to find a replacement quickly, and they were able to get hold of Charlie Calello to replace Massi's deep bass voice and bass instrument. Calello had been, up to that point, one of the Four Seasons' song arrangers, and composition was his real forte, so he played emergency short stop until the band signed bass player Joe Long to take over Massi's part permanently. However, the Four Seasons produced one of their best songs, "Working My Way Back to You" during the brief time Calello was with the band.

"Working My Way Back to You" is a lament. Narrated by a boy who kicked a nice girl to the curb, it tells the story of his change of heart and his resolve to get her back. It features both the vocal and bass-playing talents of Calello, and it is one of the Seasons' most timeless songs.

"Working My Way Back to You" is one of two songs written for the Four Seasons and Frankie Valli's voice by Denny Randell and Sandy Linzer, two new composers that Crewe brought into the Four Seasons family to add diversity to their musical canon and keep the band up to the minute.

The other song written by Randell and Linzer was "Let's Hang On." This song employed song innovative musical features that had not been heard before in the Seasons' music. Instead of an instrumental introduction, the first thing you hear in this song is Valli singing slowly and wistfully that he does not want to say goodbye. Lyrically, the song begins in the middle of the story and then flashes back to a break up conversation. The narrator (Valli, of course) pleads with his girlfriend not to end the relationship. Unlike in other Four Seasons songs, there is an admission that he has cheated on his girlfriend with another woman.

Like "Working My Way Back to You," "Let's Hang On" slotted into the rhythm and blues genre that the Four Seasons grew out of, featuring interesting bass lines and horns. As the previous hits did, it made use of Valli's falsetto and backed it up with electronic distortions that amplified the song's keening effect. It went to number three on the Hot 100 in 1965.

By 1967, Valli felt it was time to step out on his own. Though he kept working with many of the same talents that had made him famous as part of the Four Seasons machine, he was ready to take a more prominent place in the limelight. His first album, "Frankie Valli: Solo" hit the stores in 1967, and it earned Valli a new hit that more clearly showcased his solo talents than anything he had done previously. In his first real solo, "Can't Take My Eyes Off Of You," written collaboratively by Bob Crewe, Bob Gaudio, and Artie Schroeck, Valli abandoned his falsetto for a warmer, romantic sound. You might say he recovered the "angel voice" praised by his Newark neighborhood when he was still an early teen.

Valli was still attached to the Four Seasons as he would continue to be for decades to come, even though the group's roster of members changed often. Valli pursued a solo career while keeping his place in the Seasons.

In the late 1960s, the relentless touring schedule and recording sessions took their toll on Valli's vocal cords. He underwent surgery to correct the problem, but without a change in his habits, the problem was certain to recur and would have eventually wrecked his singing voice.

Frank Sinatra, of all people, came to the rescue and taught Valli the breathing techniques that empowered Sinatra to keep his voice intact and in concert form virtually up to the moment of his death.

In 1969, the band took a step that some would call a gross misunderstanding of their market and others would call a bold experiment. They released a concept album titled "The Genuine Imitation Life Gazette."

It was the psychedelic era of music. Two years previously, the Moody Blues had released "Days of Future Past." 1969 saw the release of the Beatles' "Yellow Submarine" album. The much lesser known "Genuine Imitation of Life Gazette" was similarly modeled with complex compositions that rejected the three-minute formula for radio singles and made demands on listeners' attention spans. The album cover was designed to imitate the front page of a mainstream American newspaper. The songs, too, were organized like the sections of a newspaper. Unlike the purely personal and romantic lyrics of their previous songs, "Genuine Imitation of Life Gazette" tackled political issues and current events. It referenced war and racial tensions. Valli believes it was directly influential on the Jethro Tull album "Thick As a Brick." The Rolling Stones once quipped that if "Genuine Imitation of Life Gazette" had been cut by any other band, it would have been a success.

Though Valli concedes that the album was not a commercial success and that the record company did not believe in it, he stands valiantly by the decision to make it. The Seasons, he notes, did not want to get boxed into one genre. They made the album because they loved it and wanted to do it, and they did not care whether it became a hit.

The album features the single "American Crucifixion Resurrection" which functions much like a symphony with several short movements and sweeping changes in narration and tempo. It is over six minutes long--a major departure from the usual Four Seasons formula.

Though, today, it has a loyal minority of fans on YouTube.com, in its day "Genuine Imitation of Life Gazette" came and went from the record stores without leaving much of a trace. Commercially, it was not a success.

And it came at the same time that the Four Seasons learned that one of their members, Tommy DeVito, had a serious gambling problem. If that were not bad enough, he had gambled with the band's income and failed to pay the group's taxes which brought the wrath of the IRS down on their heads.

In addition to gambling, DeVito had been profligate in his personal spending. He bought whole apartment complexes. He borrowed money which he did not repay. The other band members demanded that he make restitution, but Valli says he never did.

"We woke up one day and found that we had an incredible debt," Valli says.

Times were lean. The group was in debt and, while they still had their fan base, their solid gold run of hits had dried up. Valli says he and Gaudio were the only ones who wanted to work hard at keeping the band successful. They were the ones who went to New York every day and banged on doors while DeVito played golf and Nick DeVito slept late.

By 1970, Gaudio and Valli felt that enough was enough and they demanded that DeVito sell them his rights in the band. In exchange, they would make good on his debts and back taxes. DeVito accepted. But now the Four Seaons had lost two of the members who had produced the magic: DeVito and Massi. It was a downturn from which the group would not recover in its original incarnation.

It took years to pay off their debt. Meanwhile, the musical terrain under their feet had shifted slightly. Valli noticed that the band's music did not appeal to people who were listening avidly to Bob Dylan. The Four Seasons still played to packed out, enthusiastic audiences, but the media started giving them short shrift, suggesting they were has beens. A 1970s New York Times review of a Four Seasons concert refers to the band as "an aging quartet of relics" at the band's Carnegie Hall debut. Valli could not have been more than 36 at that time. A 1974 review in the same instrument pans the Four Seasons Madison Square Garden concert, calling it "an experiment in creeping nostalgia." It describes Valli's voice as "icy shrill" and the lyrics of the Four Seasons' songs as "nonsensical puppy love."

The early 1970s brought another change to Valli's life. He divorced Mary Mandel, his wife of thirteen years in 1971. By 1974, however, he would be remarried--this time to Mary Ann Hannigan. Their union lasted only four years, however, and was over by 1979. Valli has consistently refused to divulge information about his personal life in interviews, and little is known of his marriages or why they failed. In an interview he gave to *People Magazine* in 2008, Valli did note, "People don't get married to get divorced. Maybe people weren't meant to be together forever."

The 1970s did not consistently mistreat Valli. In fact, there were many new career highs for Valli personally, and for the Four Seasons. In 1974, emerging comedian Stewie Stone joined the Four Seasons when they performed at Bachelors III, a nightclub in Fort Lauderdale. Stone's brand of comedy complemented the Four Seasons' sound perfectly, and he went on to tour with them full time for the next four years. During that time, the hit most every nightclub in the United States, including New York's legendary Copa Cabana, Chicago's Mr. Kelly's, and Pittsburgh's Holiday House.

Stone forged a strong partnership and friendship with Valli and went on to be Valli's opening act for the next thirty years.

Valli did not forget his family or his Newark, New Jersey roots during this time. In 1971, he helped his oldest brother, Gino Chiello, open his own restaurant in East Greenwich. Gino had been a professional cook for most of his adult life when he and his two brothers started what became Mama Chiello's Restaurant on Duke Street out of their family kitchen. The restaurant became very popular and Valli often dropped by to work for a spell and relieve his brothers, both of whom became active in making the restaurant a success. The restaurant specialized in seafood, Italian dishes, and treating employees like family. It opened early every morning and did not close until 1 AM the next day. One of the brothers was always at work there.

1975 was a very good year, with successes both for the Four Seasons and for Valli's solo forays.

His solo "My Eyes Adored You" went to number one on the Hot 100, but not without a fight. This time, Valli backed himself and went to bat for his project with both barrels cocked.

"My Eyes Adored You" brought the talents of songwriter Kenny Nolan to the predictably reliable skills of Bob Crewe. They originally wrote the song for the Four Seasons and the band recorded it, but the record company (MoWest) balked at publishing it. They did not see a hit.

Valli did, though. He bought the recording for a mere $4000. He then beat on a lot of doors until Private Stock Records agreed to take it on--but only if the record label featured Valli's name alone.

The record went to the top of the chart as a Valli solo, but it also breathed new life into the Four Seasons' flagging career. They were signed with Warner Brothers Records.

In the same year, the Four Seasons published their disco-inspired "Who Loves You" album. The title song was released as a single with a B-side that featured a purely instrumental disco version of the same song. It was arguably the most successful Four Seasons recording ever with twenty weeks on the Hot 100. Valli sings lead on the verses and takes a back seat on the chorus.

In the same year, Valli's first venture into disco paid off. "Swearin To God" was a number six hit. Guy Fletcher and Doug Flett penned "Fallen Angel," which Valli sang and Gaudio produced. It fell on cool ears in the United States, but topped the chart in the United Kingdom.

Meanwhile, in the United Kingdom, Valli became a household name when the British fell in love with "You're Ready Now." Valli had recorded "You're Ready Now" ten years earlier, but it achieved little to no press in the United States. In the 1970s dance clubs of London, though, the song was a hit and went to the top of the United Kingdom music charts.

Valli produced yet another hit in 1976 with the Four Seasons. In "December, 1963" ("Oh, What a Night"), Valli shared the lead vocals with drummer Gerry Polci and bassist Don Ciccone. The song hit the top of the charts in the United Kingdom before going to the top of the Hot 100 and staying there for three weeks. It also topped Canada's RPM National Top Singles Chart.

Gaudio co-wrote the song with his wife Judy Parker. Originally, the song's lyrics celebrated the repeal of prohibition and the title was "December 5th, 1933." Valli and Parker both expressed discomfort with the lyrics, however, so it was rewritten as a memoir of a man's first love affair. Though the song's words are far from explicit, Valli later admitted the song was "about losing your cherry." "December, 1963" was the fifth and last number one hit for the Four Seasons in the United States. In many ways, "December, 1963 defined the Four Seasons as the Beatles' only true contemporary rival. The Four Seasons was the only band to have number one hits before, during, and after the Beatles career.

In 1977, the original Four Seasons formally broke up, but the band name would live on with Valli at its center and a rotating set of other members--mostly because of the group's ardent fans.

Gaudio and Valli continued as partners. Though the mainstream media had grown disrespectful of the Four Seasons, their break up precipitated a storm of disappointed fan mail. In particular, fans lamented that the group had never made a live performance album.

In response to that perceived demand, Valli and Gaudio cobbled together a new Four Seasons sound with new musicians and issued the Four Seasons' first live album, "Heaven Above Us." To replace Four Seasons members who were unavailable, they recruited Gerry Polci to play drums and sing, Jerry Corbetta to play keyboard, and Don Ciccone to play guitar. The album was recorded at a summer concert in New Jersey. By the time it was ready for distribution, Valli had undergone a change of heart. It was fun performing with the new talent. The newly-configured Four Seasons would go on to have its own career.

The Four Seasons was dead. Long live the Four Seasons.

# Chapter 4: Frankie Valli Goes Solo

From 1977 forward, Valli would pursue his own projects, singing solos in concert and records while also getting back together with the reconfigured Four Seasons when the spirit moved him.

In an interview conducted in the late 1970s, Valli said he loved performing live because it was much like a love affair. "It's very rewarding. I'm giving a piece of myself to the audience," he remarked.

He kept up an intense schedule of concerts and tours as well as recording sessions through the 1970s, despite an encroaching hearing loss that left him virtually deaf in the latter part of the decade. For many years, he had struggled with otosclerosis. His system was producing too much calcium, resulting in a hardening of the inner ear, called the stapes.

Valli was already aware he had otosclerosis when he was in his early twenties, and he had an operation in 1967 which was aimed at repairing the condition; however, the operation was unsuccessful. That left Valli with the herculean labor of performing his music in front of live audiences and keeping in sync without actually being able to hear much of the music or the beat. He kept up musically by means of memory and cranking up the volume of the music on the stage as much as he could without inducing feedback.

He underwent a second operation which also failed to restore his hearing. By 1978, he was down to twenty percent of normal function in one ear and twenty-five percent in the other.

Valli did not lose hope, though. According to a 1980 Knight News Service article, he searched the world over for a procedure that could correct his hearing loss. Finally, he found Dr. Victor Goodhill, a Los Angeles hearing specialist. Goodhill believed the best way to treat Valli was with a complete replacement of the stapes in both ears. He fashioned replacement parts out of materials he located at the University of California at Los Angeles bone bank. Valli's third surgery, in 1978, restored the majority of his hearing in one ear. A year later, Goodhill operated on the other ear and the hearing there was restored also. Valli described himself as very lucky to have his hearing back.

The restoration of Valli's hearing came just in time. In the same year, Valli got a call from songwriter Barry Gibb. Gibb was working on the film version of the successful Broadway musical *Grease*, a nostalgic story about young people growing up in a small town in the 1950s. Gibb had written a new song for the film, the title song, "Grease," and he thought Valli had the right voice to record it. Valli's manager at the time, Allan Carr, was coincidentally working on the *Grease* film production asked Valli if he wanted an acting part in the film or whether he would prefer to sing the title song. Valli, who had already fallen in love with the song the first time he heard it, opted to sing the title song. He conferred briefly with arranger Don Costa who said Valli would be crazy not to record "Grease." The acting part Valli declined was that of the Teen Angel. It was performed by Frankie Avalon who sings "Beauty School Drop Out" in one scene of the film. "Grease" went on to be a number one hit on the Hot 100 and also went to number forty on the rhythm and blues chart.

While the 1970s provided Valli with new career highs--successful solo work, a live album, the adoration of millions of fans, and a song on a smash hit movie musical, the 1980s were not so kind.

At the start of the decade, tragedy struck. Valli lost two of his daughters in the same year. Celia, his stepdaughter, was killed in a traffic accident. His daughter Francine had inherited Valli's voice, and the two of them had made plans to start performing together when she died of a drug overdose.

Valli says that he thinks about Francine every day of his life, and that the death of a child is something one never gets over.

In the same year, Valli and his fellow musicians had to cancel two shows after a bizarre accident injured several players. At an outdoor concert in Philadelphia, with no warning, a set of stage lights came crashing down onto the stage just after Valli had left the microphone. He was uninjured, but Jerry Corbetta suffered a fracture in his left hand. Toby Tyler, who was singing back up, and drummer Gerry Polci sustained cuts. Polci, who was directly under the falling lights, saved his own life by ducking underneath a raised platform.

Valli was still performing to packed audiences, often in shows that featured two or more bands from the same era. Many of the shows he performed during this time were marketed as "oldies."

The media continued to disparage his efforts on a regular basis, labelling his shows as driven by a misplaced nostalgia for the 1960s. Valli took a beating nowhere worse than in the *New York Times*. The Times coverage of a concert given jointly by Valli and the Four Tops characterized Valli's sound as flat, colorless, and void of feeling. A *Los Angeles Times* review of a concert on the same tour dismisses the Four Seasons' sound as "a worn novelty." Valli, in particular, is castigated for singing "dumb, dopey songs" about love at his age.

The reviews were not always that unkind. An article in Toronto's *Globe and Mail* praised Valli's energy and gregariousness, noting that his voice had lost none of its earlier quality and predicting that he would grace concert stages for many years yet to come. "His voice remained true to its legend," the review concluded. But loving reviews like that were not the norm.

Valli, himself, hated being classed as "nostalgia" and called people out on it in an interview with the *Orlando Sentinel*. He asked if people would classify Sinatra as "nostalgia." Or Sammy Davis, Jr., Liza Minnelli, or Luciano Pavarotti. In a 1983 interview with the *Philadelphia Inquirer*, Valli mildly defended himself against negative reviews by declaring that there were too many followers amongst music critics and not enough leaders. He noted that praising the Four Seasons was simply not "hip."

But there was no doubt that his career had lost some of its luster, just from the venues he was playing at this time. His concert tour was less about Madison Square Gardens or Carnegie Hall, venues he had played a decade earlier, and more about the Osceola County Stadium in Kissimmee, Florida, the Stabler Arena in Bethlehem, Pennsylvania, and the Ontario Place Forum in Toronto. A concert scheduled for Toronto's little-known Convocation Hall was cancelled due to poor ticket sales.

The unevenness of Valli's professional success was mirrored in his personal life. In love, he was not the luckiest guy, with two divorces under his belt by 1980, but he was not deterred from giving true love another try. In 1984, he married Randy Clohessy in St. Patrick's Cathedral in

Manhattan. The bride was twenty-four years old, and Valli was forty-seven. One hundred guests attended the wedding and a number of curious onlookers waited outside the cathedral to get a glimpse of the musical celebrity and his new bride.

Setting aside the age difference, they were a stunning couple. Clohessy wore an elaborate and sparkling bridal veil and Valli was even more dapper than usual in a cream colored, double breasted suit with lavender boutonniere. As they rode away in their gleaming Rolls-Royce toward the reception in Orange, New Jersey, Valli no doubt believed that the third time was sure to be the charm.

In 1985, Mama Chiello's Restaurant, which Valli co-owned with his brothers, was threatened with financial ruin by a fire that broke out in the basement. The restaurant had already been struggling due to nearby highway construction five years earlier. Along with his siblings, Valli took out a mortgage on his house to save the restaurant which was the love labor of Valli's eldest brother, Gino.

Through it all, Gaudio and Valli stayed true to their handshake agreement to share each other's earnings fifty/fifty. The long-standing partnership seemed to come to a sudden end in 1988 on the "Live with Regis & Kathie Lee" show. While being interviewed for that show, Gaudio and Valli got into a huge argument and canceled their deal and ended their partnership-- all on network television in front of millions of viewers. Fans were alarmed and swamped the station with calls and inquiries, but it soon turned out that the conflict was staged. And Gaudio and Valli had thought people would catch on, but they did not. News stations and newspapers set the record straight with a spate of momentary coverage.

By 1989, Valli's career got a jumpstart through an unlikely medium. He was cast in two feature films. *Eternity*, produced by Paul Entertainment's, is a time travel film, and Valli plays two characters: a medieval merchant in the film's past time frame and a television news editor in the modern era. On the heels of making "Eternity," Valli took the part of a public relations CEO in Robby Benson's film *Modern Love*.

Valli declared that an interest in acting was not just a passing whim and revealed that he had been taking acting lessons since 1963. Valli said at the time that acting in *Modern Love* had reenergized him not just for the screen, but also for music production.

In 1990, the Four Seasons received a hard-earned and overdue recognition of their talent and tenacity when the group was inducted into the Rock and Roll Hall of Fame. The award ceremony received remarkably little media coverage, but Valli was more than gracious in accepting the award on behalf of the Seasons. "Thank you very much for all the wonderful years," he said, adding "Long live rock and roll."

Valli continued to sing, record, and tour in the nineties, undaunted by an ambivalent American media which graduated from using the "nostalgia" and "oldies" labels and now just referred to Valli's sound as "grandaddy" rock.

He was still writing new music, but in his concerts, he stuck mostly to the hits that made the Four Seasons famous. It was a smart, if calculated decision that guaranteed ticket sales and a good time for all the fans of his early work.

By the early nineties, Valli had weathered numerous catastrophic financial setbacks: the debt he inherited from Tom DeVito, the fire that nearly ruined his brother's restaurant, the withheld royalties from Vee Jay Records.

Despite setbacks which would perhaps have devastated another musician, Valli came to enjoy a period of financial stability, even prosperity in the nineties that had eluded him when he was a struggling doo-wop musician in the early 1960s.

His comfortable lifestyle was by no means the product of luck. He had worked hard all his life, leveraged all his musical assets--his voice, his talent for harmonizing, his ability to put together an interesting sound with other talent. Unlike many artists, he was also conservative with his spending.

When Valli took went on tour in the United Kingdom for the first time in twelve years, a London *Daily Mail* reporter, Corinna Honan, noted that he guarded every penny.

"But boy, he's tough; a man who clearly knows how to squeeze the last dime out of a deal," Honan wrote. It was faint praise, if it was praise at all, but it does capture Valli's intelligent management of his money. Unlike so many recording artists and celebrities, Valli never fell into the trap of overspending or squandering vast fortunes on idle luxuries. And that is why he was enjoying the comfort of financial security despite the rocky path of his past career.

He had trimmed any fat off his touring budget that might cut into earnings. When he traveled the UK, he took no manager and no bodyguard with him. Valli said that he did not need a hand holder to reassure him of his talent. Nor did he need protection.

"It's terrible to go through life being frightened," was how he dismissed any concern about his personal safety.

Valli had also taken the savvy measure of buying back all the rights to his song canon along with Bob Gaudio, a move which more or less guaranteed that neither musician would end up broke in a homeless shelter while others profited from their work, a story that is far too common in the history of music.

Looming in the back of Valli's mind as a cautionary tale was the sad, but true story of Jackie Wilson, a famous rhythm and blues and soul singer who died in a hospital while on welfare, according to Valli. Despite important contributions to music, Wilson was initially placed in an unmarked grave until a fundraiser produced the money needed for a marker.

In the same year, his tour moved on to Australia. A news report on one of these concerts notes that Valli, in tandem with his new back up musicians, did a disco set, followed by music from the 1950s Variatones songbook, and then it finished up with the hits from the 1960s.

While American reviewers were cynical and dismissive of Valli's steadfast dedication to the entertainment industry, journalists in the United Kingdom and Australia yielded a grudging respect to the veteran musician, noting the longevity of his career and the strength and clarity of his singing voice. A review in Australia's *Courier-Mail* says that Valli's music is unlikely to appeal to anyone who does not remember what a 45 record is, but it allows that he gave a good show, well timed and precise.

Around this time, some prominent American celebrity musicians had been caught and lambasted for using recorded music in their concerts, lip synching in effect. The most notorious example was Milli Vanilli, a nineties band which crashed when it was discovered that the performers on stage were only pretending to sing music that had, in fact, been recorded using other, more talented artists. It soon unfolded that other musicians were also using recordings during their concerts, albeit they had recorded their own actual voices.

The bad press surrounding lip syncing may have lent new credibility to Frankie Valli and musicians like him, performers who could go anywhere in the world and give a great performance, armed only with their talent, some instruments, and a rudimentary sound amplification system. Valli shrewdly used the lip synching scandal to his benefit. In at least one concert, he noted that when he was rising in the music world there were no Milli Vanillis. Then he belted out a song in his own unblemished voice, and every note of that song was alive and in the moment.

Though he turned sixty some time in the early nineties, Valli showed no signs of slowing down. Even the most skeptical music critics could not deny that he had the energy of a fledgling musician. He was still giving 150 concerts a year, mingling with his audiences, signing autographs generously, accepting awards in person, and, whenever possible, making friends with other musicians and exchanging tips. Neither the road nor the long hard trek to fame had left a scratch on him.

It's hard to pinpoint the moment Valli's legend started snowballing in ways no one in the music industry could possibly predict. Possibly it started after he cut his greatest hits album in 1992.

The year 1993 found him accepting an award from the Parliamentary Modern Music Group in England in a ceremony attended by several Members of Parliament. MP Greg Knight pronounced Valli "one of the greatest pop singers of our time" before Valli made a tour of the House of Commons with his fans. It was one among many awards that Valli received over the years and perhaps not that extraordinary. Or maybe it signaled the beginning of a resurgence of interest in his music.

In that same year, Valli's sound found a new audience, and these were not the grandmothers reliving their golden years who had populated his audiences for the past decade or so. These were young, energetic music fans who were thronging to dance halls, dressed to the nines, and grooving to heavily percussive and remixed dance tunes. Even though "December 1963" had been remixed by Dutch music producers in the eighties, it was in 1993 that the remix became a huge dance hit.

John Garabedian, a radio show host, brought the song to America after visiting a Canadian dance club and observing nineteen-year-olds going crazy to the song. Garabedian played the song on his syndicated Open House Party show, and listeners stampeded the phone lines asking to hear it again. Not long after that, Garabedian interviewed Valli on the same show and started the interview by confessing, "I thought you were dead."

No, Valli was still very much alive, thank you. And, having weathered the adoration of millions of screaming teeny boppers in the sixties and seventies without losing his head, he was not about to lose his composure over being a dance club celebrity. The new success of his golden oldie was "a pleasant surprise," he said mildly.

The song went to number fifteen on the Billboard chart and was also a huge hit in Canada, England, and Australia. Bob Gaudio noted that a whole new generation had been turned on to the music of the Four Seasons.

In 1997, two popular feature films used "Can't Take My Eyes Off Of You" in their soundtracks. The song's wistful romantic yearning was perfect for *Conspiracy Theory*, a Mel Gibson and Julia Roberts picture in which Gibson's character obsesses over Roberts. The song was also featured in a dance scene in Sylvester Stallone's hard-hitting *Copland*.

That same year, Billboard Magazine declared the Four Seasons the "longevity champ of the rock era."

Valli had started a new family with his third wife, Randy, and the nineties found him surrounded with young children as well as two grandchildren from his first marriage. Frankie and Randy named their first son Francesco. Twin boys, Emilio and Brando, were born seven years later. It got a little noisy around the house, especially during the holidays, Valli said.

Valli's domestic happiness may have started to slip, however, in 1998 when his wife brought a small storm of negative attention to Valli's largely uncontroversial life. Valli and his wife Randy were dining at the Secret Garden restaurant in Moorpark, California with another Frankie Avalon and his wife. The two couples were outraged by the menu prices and dissatisfied with the service. The restaurant owner, Sandra "Alex" Sofsky, asked them to leave. Accounts of what transpired at this point differ. Sofsky claimed that Randy Valli became aggressive and slapped her; the Vallis maintained that Sofsky was the aggressor and that they fled the restaurant in fear. Valli's wife Randy was eventually charged and found guilty of assaulting Sofsky. Though she was not incarcerated, Randy was put on probation and sentenced to six months of community service.

Valli's concerts continued to mostly feature his Four Seasons greatest hits, though he continued to cautiously innovate, introducing a new song here, a new sound there. In one concert, he did two a cappella renditions of fifties songs, using a step ladder and garbage cans as percussion instruments.

When asked whether it was not difficult to keep playing the same tunes over and over again, for hundreds of nights in a row, years on end, he confessed that it was demanding. The secret, he said, was to remember that most people in the audience had never heard these songs live before, so it was a whole new experience for them. He referred to the Four Seasons music as a "people's act."

Valli was no stranger to television when he took a part in the controversial and award-winning *Sopranos*. He had played his music on the Ed Sullivan Show multiple times, he had been on Hullabaloo, a variety show popular in the late 1960s, and he had hosted other musical productions on TV.

He had also guest starred sporadically on earlier projects: the 1978 fantasy musical *Sgt. Pepper's Lonely Hearts Club Band*, the 1998 made-for-television movie *Witness to the Mob*, and the 1990 comedy *Modern Love*.

But this time, for his role in the *Sopranos*, he reached back into his youth growing up on the often dangerous streets of Newark. After all, the Sopranos were a crime family similar to the ones that Valli's contemporaries infiltrated, sometimes at the cost of their lives. In joining the cast of the Sopranos, Valli could leverage the mixed emotions he felt as a young man about simultaneously courting the mafia while avoiding a life of crime. Many of the little pubs and bars Valli performed in as a young man were owned by the mafia. And mob members were regular clientele of those establishments. They were a significant part of Valli's first audiences.

Valli was drawn to the program because he admired the writing of David Chase. He auditioned for the series twice. After the first audition, Chase told him he loved Valli's work, but that the role was not right for him. Chase said he would work on a way to cast Valli on the show.

Valli thought Chase was just being polite, letting him down easy. Four years later, though, Valli got a call back. Chase cast him for the show's fifth season, and Valli played the part of mafia captain Rusty Millio, a freshly released felon and member of the show's "class of 2004" as well as a family member of Carmine Lupertazzi.

Valli praises the authenticity of the show. The writing and the characters are true to the mob world he remembers as a youth. By coincidence, Valli once played in a bar owned by a mobster who went by the moniker "Pussy," and the program features a character by the same name. It is less of a coincidence that Frankie Valli is mentioned in the program. He would, of course, be a favorite of at least some crime family members.

Valli describes Millio as somewhat more polished than some of the other characters on the show, but still possessed of a tremendous potential for violence--fully capable of killing another human being.

In 2004, the press learned that Valli and his third wife, Randy, were divorcing, citing "irreconcilable differences." Valli was sixty-seven, and the couple had been together for twenty years. Divorce papers were filed in Los Angeles Superior Court. The dissolution of Valli's marriage came at almost the same moment that the new musical *Jersey Boys* would propel him back into major stardom.

# Chapter 5: Frankie Valli and The Jersey Boys

Many musicians would have been content with what they had achieved. They would have been more than happy to relax by the swimming pool, entertaining friends and fans and generally dining out on their former brilliance.

Not Frankie Valli. Valli never lost his hunger for the stage and for the process of producing music and putting on a show. Valli's love of music was one of the ingredients that propelled the musical *Jersey Boys* into the annals of great musicals.

In early 2004, script writer Rick Elice started seriously considering writing a musical about the career of the Four Seasons. Elice had connected deeply with the song "Can't Take My Eyes Off You" when he heard it in the film *Deer Hunter*. In 1979, he went to see the film multiple times, in part because he happened to be in a play with Christopher Walken who was one of the stars in *Deer Hunter*.

Elice turned to legendary scriptwriter, Marshall Brickman, whose greatest claim to fame up to that point was co-writing *Annie Hall*. Brickman's first response was to make a pun involving Vivaldi's "The Four Seasons" concertos.

His next move was to study the Four Seasons songbook, and what he found there amazed him. The story was exciting, and it was mostly virgin material as far as Broadway was concerned. Brickman, who grew up in Brooklyn, identified with Valli's strong sense of membership in the urban working class. He jumped feet first into the project of turning the band's history into a musical.

Brickman and Elice next scheduled a meeting with Valli and Gaudio.

"We had a bottle or two of wine, and they started to talk about, well, the Mafia and gambling and throwing guys through windows," Brickman said.

The wine flowed as tongues loosened, and Brickman came away with a sense that there was a story here--a story aching to be told.

Despite their stellar and lasting popularity, Brickman noted that the Four Seasons "was never really certified by the rock intelligentsia, never interviewed by *Rolling Stone*."

After their conversation with Gaudio and Valli, Brickman and Elice were even more convinced that they had a potential smash with all the right dramatic ingredients: gangsters, sex, and betrayal. Gaudio and Valli gave a nod of approval to the project.

"Take a shot and do something warts and all, and we'll decide when you go too far," Elice reports Gaudio and Valli as saying. Gaudio and Valli did not participate directly in writing the material, however. They believed they lacked the objectivity necessary to write about themselves for the production.

So Brickman and Elice got busy writing a script on spec. They encountered a great deal of resistance when they looked about for a producer, however, until they hooked up with Des McAnuff, the man who brought the musical "Tommy" to Broadway. McAnuff agreed to give the show a premier at the La Jolla Playhouse in Southern California. Now that they had an engagement and a deadline, Brickman and Elice were eager to finish their new script.

In researching and writing *Jersey Boys*, Brickman found that the three living original Four Seasons (Nick Massi had died of cancer in 2000) remembered their rise to greatness very differently, and the tales could not ultimately be reconciled. Rather than trying to merge the conflicting accounts into a definitive single story, Elice and Brickman opted to make the divergent points of view part of the story--a narrative device some have compared to the famous Akira Kurosawa film *Rashomon*. So each of the Four Seasons band members tells the story on stage the way he remembers it, and the narrative takes viewers on the journey of the Four Seasons' rise and fall. The story is interspersed with many of the band's greatest hits. Brickman and Elice admit that the show has fictional elements, but many of its scenes are taken straight out of real life.

Gaudio and Valli reserved the right to veto the project if they did not like the result which gave the script writers some trepidation. What if they put in all this work and booked a theater and actors, and then Gaudio and Valli pulled the plug? They determined it was worth the risk.

After seeing the premier, Gaudio and Valli did ask for some edits, mostly to protect the feelings of people who were still alive. But, on the whole, they loved it. Brickman praises the courage Gaudio and Valli have shown in allowing their lives to be brought to the stage.

In 2005, the musical went to New York where it was performed on Broadway. John Lloyd Young was cast in the part of Frankie Valli for the Broadway show. He did extensive research for the role. Unbeknownst to Valli, Young flew out to Las Vegas and watched Valli performed a couple of times while taking notes. Young also asked Gaudio what his first impression of Frankie Valli was; Gaudio said that he saw "a little man with a big heart."

Young could not pass for the young Frankie Valli's twin, but there are strong similarities in their appearances, especially the strong nose, slightly pointed chin, and intense eyes.

When he went to see the show's premiere in La Jolla, Valli cautioned himself against expecting that the performance would capture him exactly. Being an actor himself, he said he realized that a good performance has to be driven by something from within the actor, not something external to him.

*Jersey Boys* went on to be one of the most successful live musicals of all time, winning four Tony awards, including the award for Best Musical. In 2009, it won the Laurence Olivier Award for Best New Musical. In the two years following its first performance, it made over a hundred million dollars and another fifty million dollars in other cities where it was playing. The show has made two tours in North America. Long-term productions of the show have taken root in London, Las Vegas, Chicago, Toronto, Melbourne, Utrecht, and Singapore.

*Jersey Boys* gave a big boost to the career of the real Frankie Valli. Though he had not retired from the music scene by any means, after the runaway success of the musical about his life, Valli found himself playing to packed prestigious houses once more. In 2007, his concerts were bringing in $75,000 a night or more, and he was no longer playing to second-tier venues in concerts designed to appeal to aging rockers. Valli, now 72, rousted his audiences into enthusiastic applause by asking how many of them had seen the musical. Some of the women in the audience threw their panties on stage.

Universal Motown took timely advantage of Valli's renewed "hipness" to publish "Romancing the '60s," an album that features Valli covering standards such as "My Cherie Amour," "Sunny," "What a Wonderful World," "This Guy's in Love with You," and "Spanish Harlem." It was the first album featuring new material that Valli had released in fifteen years.

Though Gaudio and Valli had taken a back seat on the writing and producing of the original *Jersey Boys* run, they became active in 2008 and took the show to London where they oversaw its local production. In the surrounding press, Valli lavishly complimented the talents of the young actors who were playing the Four Seasons in this new production. "All of the kids who are playing these parts are spectacular! It is quite difficult for them. They have to be a triple threat, who not only have to dance and act but also sing," Valli told the *Sunday Express*.

Reviews of *Jersey Boys* attributed at least some of its success to repeat business--viewers who would pay to see the show more than once. The *Jersey Boys* was also billed as one of those rare musicals that has a strong appeal to men. They were dragging their wives to the theater for a change, instead of being dragged. Valli himself commented at how pleased he was to see whole families at the theater.

Where an unprecedented run of hit singles had failed to make Valli a fabulously wealthy man, the *Jersey Boys* succeeded. In 2011, Valli was reportedly making $515,000 a month, and the majority of that income came from *Jersey Boys* revenues.

That income became a new source of conflict for Valli and his estranged ex-wife Randy, however. Randy Valli lobbed a lawsuit at her ex-husband, demanding a greater share of *Jersey Boys* royalties. Records showed that she was, at that time, receiving $30,000 a month from Frankie and $25,000 a month in royalty payments from the show, as well as $5,000 a month in spousal support and another $810 in public assistance (a portion of Valli's Social Security benefit) because she was still raising the Valli's minor children.

The rise of *Jersey Boys* to one of the biggest grossing musicals of all time did not progress as smoothly as Valli might have hoped. Performers Christian Hoff, J. Robert Spencer, and Michael Longoria, who all had lead parts in the original *Jersey Boys* production, launched a new show that Valli and his colleagues felt too closely copied *Jersey Boys*. The former stars of *Jersey Boys* modeled their new show, *The Boys in Concert*, around the same jukebox theme of 1960s music although it covers several bands of the era, not just the Four Seasons. Valli, Gaudio, Brickman, and Elice initially said it clearly ripped off the success of *Jersey Boys'* style, stage elements, and logos. Calling it a "look alike concert," the *Jersey Boys* team demanded that the new show be canceled. They have also sued for $150,000 for each of ten songs performed in *The Boys in Concert*. The *Boys in Concert* team counter-sued, and Valli eventually dropped his suit, asking instead only that the new boys change the name of their show.

In 2010, Frankie Valli was inducted into the New Jersey Hall of Fame. His award was presented at the New Jersey Performing Arts Center in Newark by "Jersey Boys" producer Joe Grano and Bob Gaudio.

At the awards ceremony, Grano said that he had been following Valli's career and seeing him tour the country and live out of a suitcase for thirty years, and Grano had always wondered what the secret to his career's longevity was. Grano concluded that, among other things, Valli was a representative of the American dream. "Kids growing up on the street, breaking

through, even without a formal education."
Grano also praised Valli's integrity, in particular
his commitment to a partnership that was
formed without the intervention of contracts,
signatures, and lawyers.

Gaudio took the stage and took his turn
complimenting Valli. He characterized Valli as
having integrity, honesty, and fierce loyalty.

When he took the microphone, Valli said that as
a child, he lay in bed and dreamed of what his
life would become. "This is the moment I
dreamed of," he said; "To come home to New
Jersey, far beyond my own imagination a
success."

*Jersey Boys* was so fabulously successful, it was
only natural that its creative team would
consider letting it evolve into a feature film.
Warner Brothers dallied with the idea of making
the film with Jon Favreau as director, but it
never got off the ground.

In 2013, Clint Eastwood became interested in the
project. Under Eastwood's veteran direction, the
project took off. *Jersey Boys*, the movie, was
filmed that same year and scheduled for release
in June, 2014. John Lloyd Young, who played

Valli in the original stage production, reprises that performance in the film, though Young told fans of the stage version to expect some changes in the movie version. The film's other roles were cast with actors who had performed the musical live on stage, but not with the original cast members who had been involved in the litigation surrounding *The Boys in Concert*. Erich Bergen plays Bob Gaudio, Vincent Piazza plays Tommy DeVito, Michael Lomenda plays Nick Massi, Renee Marino plays Valli's first wife, who is renamed "Mary Delgado" on stage and screen, and Mike Doyle plays Bob Crewe.

The movie was filmed in Kearney, a suburb of Newark, New Jersey. Christopher Walken plays the role of Angelo "Gyp" DeCarlo, the New Jersey mafia leader who befriended Valli in his youth.

And Valli still has not retired. Who knows how many more years of performances he may have in him or what new projects are yet to unfold?

His career had highs and lows, risks and joys. Through it all, Valli never lost his love of performing for a live audience. About his career, Valli concludes, "I wouldn't change it for anything. To get out onstage and watch people get happy and appreciate what you're doing? That's like being touched by God to do something very special."

# Bibliography

Barber, R. (2011, November 10). Why Frankie's still a man for all seasons. *Daily Mail.*

BRIEFLY valli show cancelled because of poor sales. (1982, Sep 09). *The Globe and*
> *Mail* Retrieved from http://0-search.proquest.com.library.acaweb.org/advanced?accountid=13193/docview/386690081?accountid=13193

Cruz A. Frankie Valli: Oh, What a Life!. *Suzlon Energy Limited SWOT Analysis* [serial
> online]. May 26, 2008;69(20):99. Available from: Biography Reference Bank (H.W. Wilson), Ipswich, MA. Accessed May 4, 2014.

Darrow, C. (2010, September 29). Writer Tells how "Jersey Boys" Became Broadway
> Stars. *Philadelphia Inquirer.*

DeCurtis, A. (2007, September 23). Frankie Valli Is Back in Season. New York Times

Retrieved from Lexis Nexis.

Gallagher, P. (2013, July 31). Frankie Valli: Proud to Be a Jersey Boy. *Huffington Post*.

Gardner, T. (2004, March 25). Singer Frankie Valli Walks Like a Made Man. *Eugene Register-Guard*, p. 9.

Hyman, V. (2014, April 10) 'Jersey Boys' movie hits theaters June 20: 'It goes deeper,' star says. Standard Ledger Retrieved from NJ.com.

Jones, C. (2007, September 30). Frankie Valli's happy dilemma. *Chicago Tribune*.

Holden, S. (1987, Sep 20). Pop: Frankie valli and four tops share bill. *New York Times* Retrieved from http://0-search.proquest.com.library.acaweb.org/advanced?accountid=13193/docview/426611218?accountid=13193

Forum concerts canned by valli after 'act of god' frankie valli and the four seasons cancelled two performances at ontario place yesterday after three members of the singing group were hurt in an accident during an outdoor concert in phildelphia the previous night. (1980, Jul 07). *The Globe and Mail* Retrieved from http://0-search.proquest.com.library.acaweb.org/advanced?accountid=13193/docview/386933870?accountid=13193

Beck, M. (1988, Oct 10). It seems like only yesterday: Smotherses are angry at CBS.

*Orange County Register* Retrieved from http://0-search.proquest.com.library.acaweb.org/advanced?accountid=13193/docview/272211085?accountid=13193

Carlin, R. (1983, Feb 10). FRANKIE VALLISTILL SEEKING RESPECT FOR HIS

FOUR SEASONS, THE THIRD-LARGEST RECORD ACT EVER. *Philadelphia Inquirer* Retrieved from http://0-search.proquest.com.library.acaweb.org/advanced?accountid=13193/docview/293703645?accountid=13193

Fitzgerald, J. (1983, Jun 29). Valli's pipes are good for a few seasons yet. *The Globe and Mail* Retrieved from http://0-search.proquest.com.library.acaweb.org/advanced?accountid=13193/docview/386684155?accountid=13193

FRANKIE VALLI GETS TO NO 10 IN THE CHARTS (1993, March 9). Daily Mail Retrieved from Lexis Nexis Academic.

Grein, P. (1987, Oct 26). POP REVIEW FOUR TOPS, FOUR SEASONS TOGETHER AT UNIVERSAL. *Los Angeles Times (Pre-1997 Fulltext)* Retrieved from http://0-search.proquest.com.library.acaweb.org/advanced?accountid=13193/docview/292665970?accountid=13193

Honan, C. (1992, February 26). HIGH NOTES FROM HAPPY VALLI; Frankie's cashing in on the grandaddy rock boom. Daily Mail (London), Retrieved from Lexis Nexis Academic.

Jones, C. (2007, Sep 30). Frankie valli's happy dilemma; "JERSEY BOYS" IS A HUGE

HIT. BUT WHAT DO YOU DO WHEN YOUR LIFE STORY IS BIGGER BOX OFFICE THAN YOU ARE? *Chicago Tribune* Retrieved from http://0-search.proquest.com.library.acaweb.org/advanced?accountid=13193/docview/420646244?accountid=13193

Klady, L. (1989, Mar 12). Valli boy. *Los Angeles Times (Pre-1997 Fulltext)* Retrieved

from http://0-search.proquest.com.library.acaweb.org/advanced?accountid=13193/docview/280687162?accountid=13193

R. J. (1997, Nov 14). SEASONS OF RENEWAL FRANKIE VALLI SET TO RECORD

AGAIN. *The Record* Retrieved from http://0-search.proquest.com.library.acaweb.org/advanced?accountid=13193/docview/424945923?accountid=13193

Ryan. J. (1997, Nov 14). SEASONS OF RENEWAL FRANKIE VALLI SET TO

RECORD AGAIN. *The Record* Retrieved from http://0-search.proquest.com.library.acaweb.org/advanced?accountid=13193/docview/424945923?accountid=13193

Murphy, M. (2012, January 18). The boys behind "Jersey Boys". *Metro*.

Robins, W. (2013, November 7). Still working his way back to you. *Billboard, 125,*

38-42.

Shenton, M. (2008, February 17). Four Seasons veterans Frankie Valli and Bob

Gaudio reveal how their life stories were brought to the stage in the musical Jersey Boys. Sunday Express Retrieved from Lexis Nexis.

Torres Al-Shibibi, A. (1988, Sep 18). PEAKS AND DIPS FOR FRANKI VALLI POP

CROONER'S CAREER SPANS 4 DECADES OF UPS AND DOWNS.

*Orlando Sentinel* Retrieved from http://0-search.proquest.com.library.acaweb.org/advanced?accountid=13193/docview/277333649?accountid=13193

TRAFFORD, G. E. (1987, Mar 10). Brothers cook up a successful business mama

chiello can be proud of restaurateur sons. *Providence Journal* Retrieved from http://0-search.proquest.com.library.acaweb.org/advanced?accountid=13193/docview/396626609?accountid=13193

Valli Chooses New York Girl in Third Marriage. (1984, July 9). *Ocala Star-Banner*, p.

34.

VALLI'S 4 SEASONS LOUD AND WELCOME. (1970, May 12). *New York Times*

*(1923-Current File)* Retrieved from http://ezproxy.uky.edu/login?url=http://search.proquest.com/docview/119023320?accountid=11836

Yonke, D. (1998, April 27). FRANKIE VALLI IS ONE SEASON THAT NEVER

CHANGES. St. Louis Post-Dispatch
Retrieved from Lexis Nexis.

CPSIA information can be obtained at www.ICGtesting.com
Printed in the USA
BVOW06s0204171115

427433BV00024B/212/P